I wish I was a
PIRATE

by Dugald Steer Illustrated by Piers Harper

mustard

I wish I was a pirate
In pirate days of old.

I wish I was a pirate
On a hunt for pirate gold.

I'd have a pirate galleon,
I'd sail the seven seas,

I'd fly the jolly Roger,
And go just where I pleased.

I wish I was a pirate
Upon the ocean blue.

I'd have a pirate's parrot
And a jolly pirate crew.

I'd have a map and compass,
Our course would be quite plain.

I'd give my crew their orders –
"Sail for the Spanish Main!"

I wish I was a pirate
Who was just about to reach

A *pirate treasure island,*
Surrounded by a beach.

I'd stop my pirate galleon,
I'd anchor in the bay.

I'd get into the long boat,
And row there through the spray.

I wish I was a pirate.
I'd read my maps a lot.

I'd search for buried treasure,
Where X would mark the spot!

I'd find the place quite quickly,
My crew would do the rest.

They'd dig down deep until they found
A pirate treasure chest.

I wish I was a pirate,
What a fine thing to be!

I'd set sail with my treasure...

...and be home in time for tea!